a Real Life for Kids collection

Shippensburg, PA

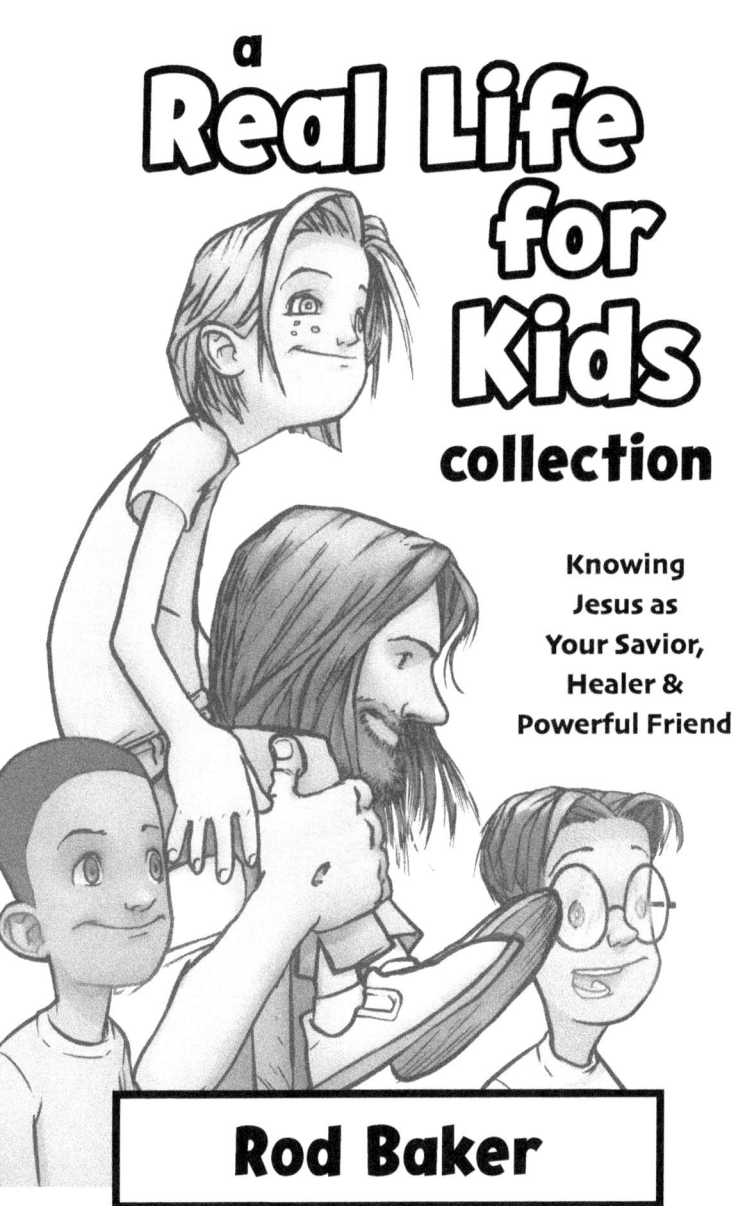

a Real Life for Kids collection

Knowing Jesus as Your Savior, Healer & Powerful Friend

Rod Baker

© Copyright 2025– Rod Baker

Printed in the United States of America. All rights reserved. No portion of this book may be reproduced, stored in a retrieval system, or transmitted in any form or by any means—electronic, mechanical, photocopy, recording, scanning, or other—except for brief quotations in critical reviews or articles, without the prior written permission of the publisher.

Unless otherwise marked, scripture references are taken from the HOLY BIBLE, NEW INTERNATION VERSION. Copyright 1973, 1978, 1984 by International Bible Society. Used by permission of Zondervan Publishing House. All rights reserved.

This Real Life for Kids collection includes the bestselling mini books: *Real Life for Kids: Knowing Jesus as Your Savior*; *Real Healing for Kids: Knowing Jesus as Your Healer*; and *Real Power for Kids: Knowing the Holy Spirit as Your Friend*. A fourth bonus book is included titled, *Giant Steps* About Growing Strong in Jesus Christ.

Giant Steps is used by permission of Victory Christian Center, Tulsa, Oklahoma.

Illustrations by Stephen Gilpin

Published by Harrison House Publishers

Shippensburg, PA 17257

ISBN 13 TP: 978-1-6675-0933-4

ISBN 13 eBook: 978-1-6675-0934-1

For Worldwide Distribution.

1 2 3 4 5 6 7 8 / 29 28 27 26 25

Contents

Dedication 9
Acknowledgments 9

REAL LIFE FOR KIDS 11

In the Beginning 12
God's Answer 16
Three in One 21
Becoming a New Creation in Christ 23
The Five Most Important Things 28
God Loves Me 29
I Have Sinned 30
God's Gift to Me 31
Jesus Died for Me 32
I Must Decide to Live for Jesus Today 33
Say It with Your Mouth 34
I Need to Tell Others About Jesus 35

REAL POWER FOR KIDS...................37

Getting Started 38

A Promise from God 40

The Holy Spirit Comes..................... 41

Speaking in Tongues 43

It Is a Free Gift........................... 44

How to Receive the Power of the Holy Spirit . . . 47

Every Day with the Holy Spirit 50

What Praying in Tongues Does............... 52

Finishing Strong 59

REAL HEALING FOR KIDS 61

Getting Started 62

God Wants Us Healed..................... 64

Sickness Comes from the Devil 67

Jesus Paid the Price 70

Steps to Healing 72

Faith Pleases God 75

Speaking God's Word 77

When It Seems Like You're Not Getting Better—
Don't Give Up 79
Good-Bye Sickness 81
Daily Confessions for Healing 83

GIANT STEPS 85

Introduction 86
You Are a Giant 87
Your New Life in Christ.................... 90
You Have a Heavenly Father................ 97
Filled with the Holy Spirit................. 104
A Life of Blessings 109
A Life of Victory 114
You Have a Purpose......................119

About the Author 127

Dedication

To Amber—my winner!

Acknowledgments

Thank you to my wife, Gloria, who is the glory of my life; to my granddaughters, Gigi and Winner; and to the children of the world!

REAL LIFE FOR KIDS

KNOWING JESUS AS YOUR SAVIOR

In the Beginning

In the beginning, God created the heavens and the earth. When He saw how wonderful everything was, He created man and woman and put them in a beautiful garden called Eden, where they could enjoy the things He had created. The garden was a perfect place to live with everything they needed.

Every day God walked and talked with the man and woman whom He called Adam and Eve. God's plan was for them and their family to live with Him forever in this perfect place.

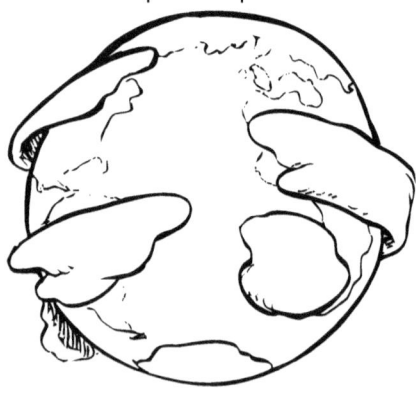

God told Adam and Eve they could eat anything they wanted in the garden except for the fruit of one tree.

But looking like a snake one day, the devil came into the garden and tricked them into eating fruit from the tree God had told them not to eat from. When Adam and Eve ate the fruit, they disobeyed God and were no longer perfect.

Disobedience to God is called sin.

And since God is perfect, He cannot live with sin. Adam and Eve had to leave the garden because their sin separated them from God and His perfect plan for their lives.

God's plan back then and today is that people would walk in the good life that He creates for them and ultimately live with Him forever. But the devil lies and tricks people into thinking sin is more attractive. The truth is, the devil really brings them sickness and sadness, and eventually when they die, he tortures them forever in hell.

Yet God loves people so much He cannot stand to be separated from them, and that's why He

Real Life for Kids

designed an awesome plan to bring people back to Him.

God decided that the only way to save man from sin was to send His only Son, Jesus, to earth to live as a man, perfect and without sin. As a perfect man, He would die to pay for all sin of all people.

For God so loved the world that He gave His one and only Son, so that whoever believes in Him shall not perish (die), but have eternal life.

John 3:16

God's Answer

God loves us so much that He designed a plan for us to escape the punishment we deserved for our sins. God's plan was that Jesus would take the consequences, or punishment, for sin that should have been ours.

Jesus willingly cooperated with God's plan even though He lived a perfect life. Even though the devil tried to trick Him, just like he does everyone, Jesus never fell for his tricks and He never once sinned. He never did anything wrong and did not deserve to die.

Jesus chose to die on the cross and pay for the sin of all people with His blood. The Bible says in Hebrews 9:22 that "without the shedding of blood there is no forgiveness." Jesus' perfect blood was the only thing that could pay for our sin.

Knowing Jesus as Your Savior

You might wonder why He would die for a sinner or for someone who may not even like Him. The answer is love.

God sees us as His children, and it hurts Him to see us suffer. So, instead of our having to suffer and die, He sent Jesus to take our place so that we could live.

First Corinthians 15:3-4 (KJV) says, "How that Christ died for our sins according to the scriptures; and that He was buried and that He rose again the third day according to the scriptures."

We are saved by grace. Ephesians 2:8 (KJV) says, "For by grace are ye saved through faith; and that not of yourselves: it is the gift of God." Grace can be described as God being kind even when we don't really deserve it.

No one deserves to be saved. And no one can earn salvation by doing good things. The truth is, we receive salvation through faith in God when we do two things. First, we must believe in our hearts that Jesus died for us and God brought Him back to life; and second, we must say with our mouths that Jesus is Lord, or boss, of our life. (Rom. 10:9,10.)

God gives us a choice—we can either serve Him or the devil. He never forces us or makes us do anything. The choice is ours to make.

If you want to be saved and live to serve God, pray this prayer and believe it.

> Father, I believe that Jesus died on the cross for my sins. I believe that He rose from the dead so that I can live with Him forever. I ask You to forgive me of my sins. I ask You to come into my heart and be the Lord (boss) of my life. I confess with my mouth that I am born again.

Thank You for saving me. Amen.

If you prayed this prayer and believe it in your heart—wow—you have just made the most important decision of your whole life!

You are saved from the devil and his way of life, and you are now born again into God's family. You are a new creation. (2 Cor. 5:17.)

You still look the same as before you prayed. You're just as tall and weigh the same; your hair and eye color didn't change. But you changed plenty on the inside. Let's find out what's new with you—and Who and what you received.

Three in One

God is a three-part person. He is the Father, the Son, and the Holy Spirit, yet He is still One.

God made man in His image. So we are a three-part person, too. We are a spirit, we have a soul, and we live in a body.

You cannot see your spirit, but it is the real you. It is the part of you that lives forever. The spirit man is the part of you where the Spirit of God makes His home. The Spirit of God lives in your spirit.

Your soul is the part of you that makes decisions, feels emotions like love or sadness, and where your personality comes from. It's a combination of your mind, will, and emotions.

Finally, you live in a body. The body is that beautiful creation you see every day when you look in the mirror.

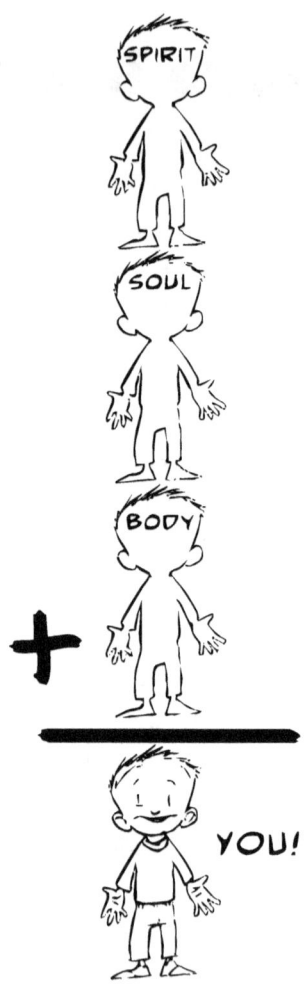

Becoming a New Creation in Christ

Second Corinthians 5:17 (KJV) says, "Therefore, if any man be in Christ, he is a new creature."

When we receive Jesus as our Savior, we get a brand-new spirit. God doesn't just clean and polish the old one; we get a brand-new one. That's what it means to be born again.

When we're born again, we get a new spirit that is perfect like God's. Our old way of doing things and thinking are replaced with wanting to do things God's way.

But our souls don't get saved, so we need to make our minds new by reading and studying God's Word. It's His Word that makes our minds think more like God thinks. (Rom. 12:2.)

Our body does not get saved either. But, as we make our mind new, it's easier to obey God and live for Him because our spirit, soul, and body will be working together to serve God.

God wants everyone to be born again (saved). (1 Tim. 2:4.) And it's His plan for us to spend time with Him not only here on earth but also forever in heaven.

It's important to spend time with God—like you do with your friends. You probably spend a lot of time with your best friend from school or your neighbor. You probably know all his or her favorite things or things they don't like. If your friend called on the phone and said hello but didn't say his or her name, you would still know the voice because you know your friend.

And that's the way it needs to be with God. He wants to be our best friend, too. (Prov. 18:24.)

The more time we spend with Him by praying or reading our Bible, the better we get to know Him. We learn what He likes and does not like for our lives. We know when He's telling us to do something and not the devil. We know Him just like we know our best friend from school.

Yet, God is better than our best friend from school because He will never disappoint us or let us down. He will never break a promise or lie to us. He is always ready to listen and help us when we need it.

To know Him as your best friend every day you need to:

Read your Bible: A good place to start is with the book of John in the New Testament.

Pray: This is just talking and listening to God like you would your friend.

Praise Him: Tell Him how much you love Him and are thankful for what He does.

Knowing Jesus as Your Savior

1. Read

2. Pray

3. Praise

The Five Most Important Things

Before a person can be saved, he or she needs to understand the five most important things in the world.

Here is an easy way to understand and remember the Gospel so you can share it with others every chance you get.

Knowing Jesus as Your Savior

God Loves Me

For God so loved the world that He gave His one and only Son, that whoever believes in Him shall not perish but have eternal life.

John 3:16

I Have Sinned

For all have sinned and fall short of the glory of God.

Romans 3:23

Knowing Jesus as Your Savior

God's Gift to Me

For the wages of sin is death, but the gift of God is eternal life in Christ Jesus our Lord.

Romans 6:23

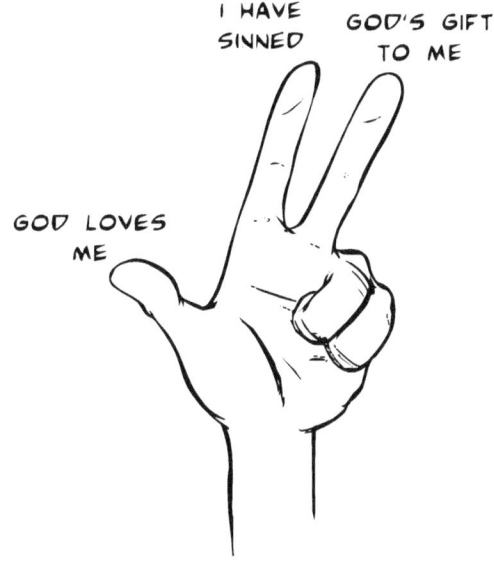

Jesus Died for Me

...How that Christ died for our sins according to the scriptures.

1 Corinthians 15:3 (KJV)

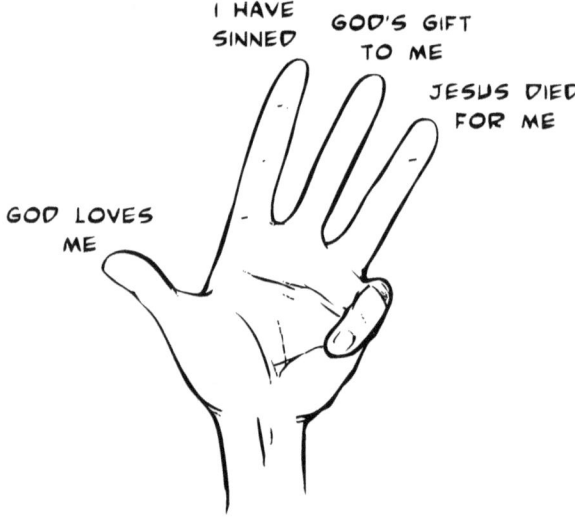

Knowing Jesus as Your Savior

I Must Decide to Live for Jesus Today

I tell you, now is the time of God's favor, now is the day of salvation.

2 Corinthians 6:2

Say It with Your Mouth

That if you confess with your mouth the Lord Jesus and believe in your heart that God has raised Him from the dead, you will be saved. For with the heart one believes unto righteousness, and with the mouth confession is made unto salvation.

Romans 10:9,10 (NKJV)

Knowing Jesus as Your Savior

I Need to Tell Others About Jesus

Go into all the world and preach the good news to all creation.

Mark 16:15

REAL POWER FOR KIDS

KNOWING THE HOLY SPIRIT AS YOUR FRIEND

Getting Started

The Holy Spirit is a gift from God to you—and everyone who accepts Jesus as his or her Savior. He will be your helper to guide you and help you know how to pray. He will comfort you when you feel afraid or alone.

Read along, and we will walk you through every step you need to take to receive the power of the Holy Spirit.

Knowing the Holy Spirit as Your Friend

A Promise from God

The gift of the Holy Spirit has been promised by God for a long time. John the Baptist preached about it. Jesus told His disciples about the Holy Spirit. Before Jesus returned to heaven after His work on earth, He told them to wait in the city of Jerusalem until they received power from heaven.

That is exactly what they did. On the day of Pentecost, one hundred and twenty men were all praying. They were praying the same thing. They were praying for the promise of the Holy Spirit.

The Holy Spirit Comes

Suddenly, there was a sound like a mighty rushing wind. Something that looked like fire appeared in the room and landed on each person. When that happened, they were all filled with the Holy Spirit and began to speak with an unknown language as the Spirit gave them the words to say.

The Holy Spirit filled all the people in the room. No one was left behind. Everyone received the promise. The Holy Spirit works the same way today. Everyone can receive.

The disciples left the Upper Room in power. From that moment on, they were changed. They spoke in the temple. They preached from prisons. They healed the sick and the lame. It was like Jesus was there again doing the miracles, but this time, God was using His Holy Spirit-filled disciples.

You can receive the power of the Holy Spirit. You can have the same power that they had in the Bible. God has made sure that every person has been given the gift. It's yours for the taking. All you need to do is accept Jesus as your Savior and receive the gift by faith.

Speaking in Tongues

The day of Pentecost was the first time ever that the Holy Spirit filled believers to speak with other tongues. After that, there were many more times groups of people received the power of the Holy Spirit. Each time they did, speaking in an unknown language, or tongues, was present. It was the evidence, or proof, that people had received the power of the Holy Spirit. You will speak in other tongues, too, when you receive the power of the Holy Spirit.

It Is a Free Gift

Anything that God has for you is free. Free! Absolutely free. You couldn't pay for it if you wanted to. That is because Jesus already paid the price for every gift you need. Salvation is free! Healing is free! The gift of the Holy Spirit is free, too!

You cannot earn it or pay for it. It's free! All you need to do is accept it.

It's like this. On your birthday your parent gives you a present. You don't have to work for your present. You don't have to beg for your present. You just receive it because it was bought for you.

Receiving the power of the Holy Spirit is the same way. God is handing you a gift. You don't beg or talk God into it. You just reach out and receive it. And it's that easy because it belongs to you.

Knowing the Holy Spirit as Your Friend

How to Receive the Power of the Holy Spirit

You don't need to pray for a long time asking God to give you the power of the Holy Spirit. Remember, the gift is already yours. You are just receiving what is yours to begin with.

The Holy Spirit has a part to do and you have a part to do. As the Holy Spirit fills you, He gives you the words to say. It's the Holy Spirit's job to give you the language or words to say.

Your part is to open your mouth and speak those words or sounds or languages. You may make one sound or maybe many different sounds. This is what we call "other tongues" or an "unknown language." You resist the desire to talk in English and yield or give way to the words the Spirit is giving you. It's not something in your mind, but something that comes from down in your spirit man.

You can pray to receive the Holy Spirit anywhere. In fact, believe you receive when you pray and it will be done for you. Remember your part: you do the talking. The Spirit does the filling. When you begin to speak your new language, it may seem strange at first but stick with it.

Here is a prayer to help you:

Father, the Bible promises that I can receive the free gift of the Holy Spirit. You want me to have it more than I do. I ask You in the name of Jesus to fill me with Your Holy Spirit, and I receive it now. Thank You, Father God. Amen.

Every Day with the Holy Spirit

Now that you have received this wonderful gift from God, you need to make it a part of your everyday life. You can pray at any time or any place you want to. You can pray in tongues beside your bed, on your way to school, playing in the park, standing on your head, or even in the shower. Wherever and whenever you want to, you can do it.

Don't be concerned that you only speak a few words in other tongues. As you pray more, more words appear in your language. It takes some time. Be patient.

You won't understand these words either. That's okay. The Bible says that when we pray in other tongues, we speak mysteries in the spirit. Our minds are not aware and don't understand the meaning of what our spirits are praying to

God. Yet the Bible says that your prayers in other tongues are prayed perfectly and delivered to God.

The devil will try to steal the Word of God from your heart. He will try to tell you that you didn't really receive the power of the Holy Spirit. He will tell you that you are just making this up yourself. But remember, he is the father of lies. And if that is the case, then he must be lying to you as well. Just go back to God's Word and remember that God promised this gift to you.

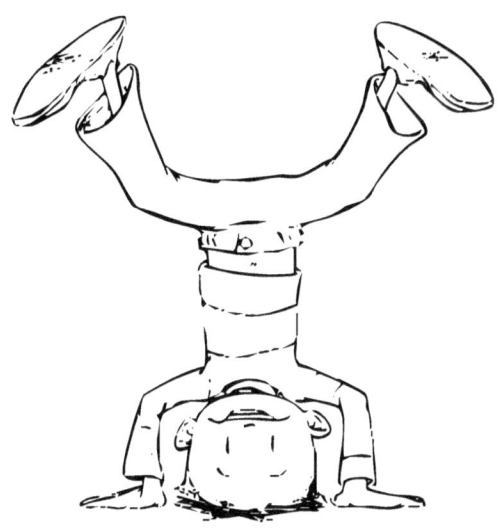

What Praying in Tongues Does

Helps us remember that God is always with us.

Speaking in tongues is a great way to stay aware of God in our everyday life. We feel comfortable and secure knowing He is with us all the time. (Heb. 13:6.)

Allows the Holy Spirit to help us.

The Holy Spirit is our helper. He has been called alongside us to help. The Holy Spirit is not doing the praying; we are. Yet He is helping us. That means more of our prayers are being answered. (John 14:16 NAS.)

Helps us know what to pay about.

There are times that we cannot think of how to pray. Our minds cannot think the problem out. Yet, thank God, the Holy Spirit knows all truth and leads our spirit in the exact prayer that is right for the situation. (Rom. 8:26.)

Helps us pray according to God's will.

Sometimes on their own people don't pray God's will. They don't do it on purpose, they just don't know the right way to pray. But the Holy Spirit searches the mind of God, prays according to His will, and leads you in a prayer that always works. (Rom. 8:27.)

Helps us increase our faith.

The Bible tells us that we build up ourselves on our most holy faith, praying in the Spirit. It's like the Holy Spirit supercharges our faith when we pray in tongues. It would be like trying to cut a limb of a tree with a saw. It might take you until dinner time to get done sawing. But if you break out the chainsaw, you will be done before you break a sweat. (Jude 1:20.)

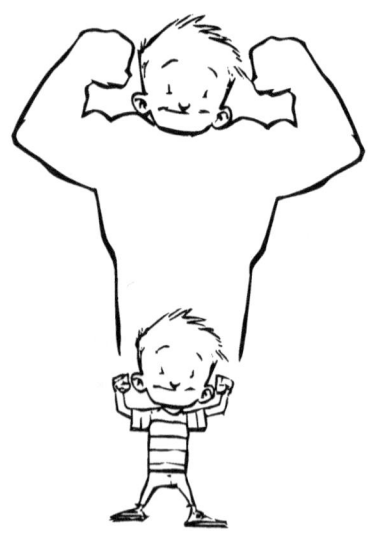

Builds your spirit up.

As a kid I used to love playing with battery-operated toys until the batteries began to get low. The toys would slow down and lose their power. We are like that, too. When we spend a lot of time giving to the work of God, our spirits get weaker like a battery does in a toy. Praying in tongues helps us to recharge our batteries. Praying in other tongues builds us up in every area of our lives. (Jude 1:20.)

Helps you pray about the future.

One of the jobs of the Holy Spirit is to show us "things to come." When we pray in tongues, we can get a sneak preview of what God is about to do. Now, you won't know who will win the Super Bowl in advance, but you can understand what's coming ahead for your life. (Jer. 29:11.)

Finishing Strong

History is full of examples of what men and women full of the Holy Spirit have been able to accomplish for God. You can accomplish great things, too! Pray often in the Spirit, and you will see your life in Christ grow beyond your wildest dreams. It's up to you. When you pray in tongues, the impossible becomes possible.

Share this precious gift with your friends. This gift is for everyone, from the new believer to those who have been Christians for a long time. This gift

is for the Charismatic churches, the Methodists, the Catholics, the Baptists, the Presbyterians, and the list goes on and on. If someone knows Jesus as his or her Savior, the person should know the Holy Spirit as a helper as well as a power source to help the person do what God wants him or her to do.

REAL HEALING FOR KIDS

KNOWING JESUS AS YOUR HEALER

Getting Started

Nobody likes to be sick. Nobody likes that terrible, queasy feeling in their stomach or their head pounding with a fever. Everybody hates coughing, sneezing, and runny noses. And worse yet, some people have more serious sicknesses and diseases like cancer or heart problems. In fact, sickness can make life hard because it keeps people from serving God, going to school, working, and having fun.

But know this: It's not God's plan for you to be sick!

If you know and believe in your heart that God wants you to be well, you'll know what to do when sickness comes your way you'll know how to receive healing that already belongs to you.

Use this book to learn about healing. Read it every now and then to make sure you've got the basics down. You can even use this book to help your friends learn more about how God wants to heal them, too.

God Wants Us Healed

It doesn't matter to God whether you have a big, serious disease that threatens your life or a plain old stomachache. No matter, God wants to heal you. He never says no to healing. He is never too busy to answer your prayer. And His answer to healing is always yes.

The best way to understand how much God wants to heal you is to look at His Word, the Bible. In Psalm 107:20 God says, "He sent out his word and healed them." He says in Exodus 15:26, "I am the Lord, who heals you." These Scriptures are just two of many promises God has given everyone of us for healing.

In the Bible, He told the children of Israel that if they would listen and obey Him, none of them would even be sick. In fact, when they left Egypt

for the Promised Land there wasn't a sick person in the whole group of 3 million people.

You can count on the fact that if God makes a promise, it's a done deal. God the Father always keeps His promises. That's why we can read His Word and believe it. If He said it, it will happen. Period.

Real Healing for Kids

Sickness Comes from the Devil

Have you ever wondered where sickness came from?

Some people believe that because God created everything, He also created sickness. But that's not true. He did not.

Some people believe that God uses sickness to teach His children a lesson—like a parent spanking a child. Even more, there are people who believe that God chooses not to heal some sick people right away so the sick person can get stronger in his or her faith and bring God more glory. What a silly thought!

God did not create sickness. He does not use sickness to teach us a lesson or to bring Him glory. Sickness is from the devil.

The Bible makes this all very clear in John 10:10 by telling us what the devil's job is, and what Jesus' job is. It says, "The thief (the devil) comes only to steal and kill and destroy; I (Jesus) have come that they may have life, and have it to the full." The difference is like night and day. The devil harms us; Jesus blesses us.

The devil's job is to "steal." He tries to steal your fun, your joy, and your health. If the devil can, he will try to take your life altogether. His job is to destroy the work of God on this earth. But don't be afraid; even the weakest Christian has power over the devil. The Bible says that "greater is he (God) that is in you, than he that is in the world." (1 John 4:4 KJV.)

The good news is that you don't have to take sickness from the devil. James 4:7 says, "Submit yourself, then, to God. Resist the devil, and he will flee from you." When you start to feel sickness in your body, refuse to accept the sickness with the Word of God. If you do this, each time the devil tries to put sickness or disease on you, it will not stick. That way you can stay healthy.

Knowing Jesus as Your Healer

Jesus Paid the Price

Long ago, Jesus left heaven, came to earth, and paid for your healing with His own body so you could be well every day of your life.

How did He pay the price for healing? Just before Jesus was crucified on the cross, Roman soldiers beat Jesus terribly with whips and sticks. With great force soldiers hit His back, each time tearing the skin and leaving a mark called a stripe. Each of those stripes paid for your healing.

The Bible says in Isaiah 53:5 (NKJV) that "By His stripes we are healed." If God did not want us to be healed, Jesus would never have suffered for us that way. He paid too great a price not to heal us when we ask.

The Bible tells us that everywhere Jesus went He did three things. He preached, He taught the people, and He healed the sick. And everywhere He went, the lame walked, the deaf heard, the blind saw, and the dead were raised to life.

What worked in Bible days will work for you today because Hebrews 13:8 says, "Jesus Christ is the same yesterday and today and forever." If Jesus healed people in the past, He will do it today, and He will still be healing people tomorrow.

There is not one record in the Bible that Jesus ever gave someone sickness. There isn't one place where Jesus ever refused to heal someone who believed for healing.

Steps to Healing

Do you need to receive healing? First of all, you must believe that Jesus has already paid the price for your healing. It is a free gift. You do not have to plead or beg for it. It belongs to you. When faith touches God, God will touch you, and you will be healed.

If you or someone you know is sick, you can receive healing in any of the following ways.

You can say:

1. In the name of Jesus, sickness leave my body.

Every believer—kids too—has been given authority (power) over the devil. If you demand in faith that sickness leave, the devil must pack up sickness and go! (Luke 10:19.)

2. Lord, thank You for healing me, in Jesus' name.

First Peter 2:24 (NKJV) says, "Who Himself bore our sins in His own body on the tree, that we, having died to sins, might live for righteousness—by whose stripes you were healed."

Just believe in your heart that you are healed, and healing will be yours.

3. I agree with you that you're healed in Jesus' name.

Matthew 18:19 says "If two of you on earth agree about anything they ask for, it will be done for them by my Father in heaven."

Faith Pleases God

Healing is easy to receive, but there are two things you must believe.

The first thing you must believe is that God is a powerful God and He is *able* to heal you. The second thing you must believe is that God *wants* to heal you.

You cannot have any doubt about it! Your act of trusting and believing God is what the Bible calls faith. And even though God wants you healed even more than you want to be healed, you still have to trust Him and have faith.

In fact, faith begins where the promises of God are understood. Amazingly, God's Word becomes alive in your spirit and produces a force called faith. And faith is the one thing in the whole world that causes God to act or create in your life the very thing you trust Him for.

It's important to understand that faith works in your heart not your head. Just because you think something in your head, it does not mean you believe it in your heart. You might decide in your mind that God can heal and wants to heal, but until that decision drops from your head to your heart, it's not faith.

So how do we get faith? Romans 10:17 (NKJV) says, "So then faith comes by hearing, and hearing by the Word of God." That means if we need faith for healing, we can read God's Word to get it. Even a little faith does a lot.

Speaking God's Word

After you hear God's Word and faith rises in your heart, it's important to release that faith to work for you. Speaking the Word of God gives power to your words. Those faith-filled words can change things and even receive healing for you.

Romans 10:8 says, "'The word is near; it is in your mouth and in your heart,' that is, the message concerning faith that we proclaim."

You can speak the Word of God to sickness and you will receive healing. Jesus said, "if you do not doubt in your heart but believe what you speak," it will happen just as you say.

Say Scriptures about healing out loud. Speak them boldly and often. Your faith will grow stronger each time you do.

Another way we use our faith and our words is when we resist the devil. That means we refuse to accept the devil's lies about being sick. Remember, James 4:7 tells us "to resist the devil, and he will flee from you." We resist him by speaking the Word of God.

When you begin to feel sick, speak the Word instead of talking about how sick you feel. Don't talk sickness; talk the Word. Begin to say, He (Jesus) took my sicknesses and diseases, and by His stripes I am healed. If you resist the devil, he must flee! You've got God's Word on it.

Signs of sickness are the devil's lies. If he can get you to believe your aches and pains instead of the Bible, he can steal your health. When that happens, you become sick. Just remember—the devil is a liar and the father of all lies. Don't focus on how you feel. Instead, focus on God's Word and His promises of healing to you! You'll find many confessions of healing in the back of this book.

When It Seems Like You're Not Getting Better— Don't Give Up

Sometimes you don't feel like you are healed when you first pray. Don't give up. Don't worry. Hold on to your confession of faith. Healing belongs to you, and you will receive it. Keep believing!

When healing does not come like we expect, we need to look at our life to see why. It is not God's fault; He absolutely wants to heal you.

Maybe you didn't receive healing when you first prayed

because you have disobeyed God, or maybe you are just hoping instead of truly believing.

If you have disobeyed God, simply ask God to forgive you, start obeying, and then receive your healing. If the problem is your faith, go back to reading and confessing the Word of God, charge up your faith, and keep standing in faith.

No matter what, don't give up.

Good-Bye Sickness

There is no doubt that God has the power to heal even the hardest of diseases. Yet did you know that He can also help keep you from getting sick? Sure, He can. It is called divine health. You can live the rest of your life without ever getting sick again.

God's plan for a believer is to be healthy. It is the devil's job to steal that from you. If you have faith in God, He will protect you from attacks.

Reading God's Word every day will build your faith. The Bible says that God's Word is like a medicine. If you read the Bible daily, the Word acts like a medicine to keep away the attacks of sickness that normally come. You will stay healthy.

Your lifestyle also has a lot to do with your wellness. All of the experts agree that the proper diet, combined with exercise and the right amount of sleep, will help keep people strong and healthy.

Do not put bad things in your body like tobacco, alcohol, or drugs. It is proven that these things hurt your body and make it weak so it is easier for the devil to attack you with sickness.

Practice good hygiene. Take baths and wash your hands often to prevent the spread of everyday diseases.

If you do these things, you will remain free of sickness and disease. Do them all in faith and God will partner with you in healing and in health.

Daily Confessions for Healing

Jesus said that if I can believe, all things are possible; so I believe that I am healed.

Mark 9:23

It is God's plan that I would be healthy in my soul and in my body; so as my faith grows I am healthy.

3 John 2

I believe that the same Spirit that raised Jesus from the dead lives in me and He has healed my body.

Romans 8:11

God has saved me from the hand of the enemy. I believe and say that I am saved from the sickness of the enemy.

Psalm 107:2

God sent His Word to heal me. I have received His Word, so I am healed.

Psalm 107:20

He is the Lord that heals me. I am healed.

Exodus 15:26

I pay attention to the Word of God, and it is life and health to me.

Proverbs 4:20-22

By the stripes of Jesus I am healed.

1 Peter 2:24

Jesus took on Himself my sickness, so I do not have to be sick.

Matthew 8:17

I will praise the Lord who healed all of my diseases.

Psalm 103:1-3

GIANT STEPS

Introduction

Hi! I want to tell you that I'm really happy that you decided to live for Christ. This book will help you to grow and give you steps to be like a GIANT in your new life.

Your Friend...

Rod Baker

You Are a Giant

A long time ago a boy named David was sent to the battlefield to check on his older brothers. When David got there, a very loud voice was heard. The Philistines were on one hill, and the people of God, the Israelites, were on the other. In the middle of the valley was a giant Philistine named Goliath, who was more than three meters tall.

While holding a large sword, Goliath asked in a loud, booming voice, "Who will dare to fight against me?" All the Israelite soldiers were afraid of him, except David. David walked to the battlefield with just a sling and five stones. Goliath shouted to him, "I'm going to kill you!" David looked straight at Goliath and said, "I come against you in the name of the Lord God Almighty."

When Goliath came to attack him, David ran to face him. David put a stone in his sling and threw it right at Goliath's forehead. The giant fell to the ground. David defeated him! He was just a little boy...but he defeated a giant!

Even though David was a boy, he was a giant in God's eyes because he knew God could give him the power to defeat the enemy.

In this book, you will find out how to become a GIANT just like David.

"For God so loved the world that he gave his one and only Son, that whoever believes in him shall not perish but have eternal life."

John 3:16

"…and I no longer live, but Christ lives in me…."

Galatians 2:20

"So if the Son sets you free, you will be free indeed."

John 8:36

"In him and through faith in him we may approach God with freedom and confidence."

Ephesians 3:12

Your New Life in Christ

"For God so loved the world that he gave his one and only Son, that whoever believes in him shall not perish but have eternal life."

John 3:16

A. You must be born again

Did you know that Jesus went to heaven to prepare a very special place for you? Heaven is beautiful, and God lives there. However, there is something that you have to know: You can't go to heaven just because you go to church, pray a lot, or just because you are a good person. To go to heaven you must receive Jesus in your heart and be born again.

> "Jesus replied, "Very truly I tell you, no one can see the Kingdom of God unless they are born again."
>
> **John 3:3**

Do you know something? We all have done bad things, such as lying or stealing. That sin pushes us away from God. But there is GOOD NEWS…God has the solution! He paid for your sin when He sent His only Son to die on the cross. God is not mad at you for the sins you have done. He loves you, and He made a path to save you. He gave you the greatest gift of all, His Son, Jesus.

It's your decision to receive Him. There is no other way to go to heaven, only through Jesus.

> "Jesus answered, 'I am the way and the truth and the life. No one comes to the Father except through me.'"
>
> **John 14:6**

At the moment you believe in your heart and confess with your mouth that Jesus is Lord...you are born again!

B. You are a new creation

To be born again makes you a new person.

> "Therefore, if anyone is in Christ, the new creation has come: The old has gone, the new is here!"
>
> **2 Corinthians 5:17**

On the outside, your body is the same, but inside you are new. God has thrown away any mistake and failure in your past; He has cleansed you and now He lives in you. In your heart you have been made to be like Jesus. Now you are a new person ready to walk with God.

> "…and I no longer live, but Christ live in me…."
>
> **Galatians 2:20**

"So if the Son sets you free, you will be free indeed."

John 8:36

Stand up in the truth of God and believe that you are free!

C. Freedom in Christ

Would a prisoner remain in his cell if the door were unlocked? No! he would walk to freedom. Jesus has delivered you from the devil's trap; do not remain a prisoner.

The Bible says, "...the thief comes only to steal and kill and destroy..." (John 10:10). Satan wants to destroy your life, but Jesus says, "...I have come that they may have life, and have it to the full" (John 10:10).

You don't have to live in fear, poverty, sin, or sickness. Jesus gave His life...you can be free!

D. Your personal relationship with Jesus

The wall of sin that separated you from God is now destroyed. You can have a personal relationship with Jesus. You are not a stranger to God.

> "Consequently, you are no longer foreigners and strangers, but fellow citizens with God's people and also members of his household."
>
> **Ephesians 2:19**

You are a child of God. Does a loving father ever turn away when his child comes looking for a hug? No! He is ready to hug his child with love. So you can go directly to God, knowing that He loves you and He is waiting for you.

God talks to you through His Word and His Holy Spirit who is in you. He wants to be your friend!

"In him and through faith in him we may approach God with freedom and confidence."

Ephesians 3:12

"For I know the plans I have for you…plans to prosper you and not to harm you, plans to give you hope and a future."

Jeremiah 29:11

"The Lord is my shepherd, I lack nothing."

Psalm 23:1

"Though my father and mother forsake me, the Lord will receive me."

Psalm 27:10

You Have a Heavenly Father

A. You are a child of God

"Yet to all who did receive him, to those who believed in his name, he gave the right to become children of God."

John 1:12

When you allow Jesus to become your Lord and Savior, you become a child of God. You are worthy and special to God. He made you unique, and He has a wonderful plan for your life.

"For I know the plans I have for you…plans to prosper you and not to harm you, plans to give you hope and a future."

Jeremiah 29:11

He loves you, and He wants you to have the best in life. Your heavenly Father has given you the rights to all He has. You are an heir of the Maker of the universe! So if you live for God, you will have rights to all His benefits.

B. Jesus is the Good Shepherd

"The Lord is my shepherd, I lack nothing."

Psalm 23:1

A good shepherd loves and knows each one of his sheep. He guides them to water and food. The shepherd protects them with his staff; and if a wolf gets close, he risks himself to save his sheep. Sheep learn that they have to be close to the shepherd to remain alive.

We are people in a big world. Sometimes you feel alone or scared, but you don't have to be afraid. Jesus is the Good Shepherd! He guides us through life and protects us from the enemy. Jesus will always be with you no matter what happens. If you are close to Jesus, the Good Shepherd, you don't have to be afraid.

"My sheep listen to my voice; I know them, and they follow me."

John 10:27

C. God knows where you are and the things that happen to you

Your life is so precious to God. His eye is on you at all times.

> "He who watches over you will not slumber.... The Lord will watch over your coming and going...."
>
> **Psalm 121:3,8**

God knows when you sit, when you rise, and even what you are thinking (Psalm 139:1,2). He even knows how many hairs are on your head (Matthew 10:30). God cares about you! His thoughts of you are more than the grains of sand (Psalm 139:17,18).

You are important to Him!

D. The Father's love for you

Do you know how much the heavenly Father loves you! There is no bigger love than the love He has for you. "Greater love has no one than this: to lay down one's life for one's friends" (John 15:13). You were beautifully made and are precious before His eyes. His eyes are upon you all the time. He knows your thoughts and where you are; He understands what is happening in your life.

It might be difficult for you to believe that someone loves you that much; maybe you have never been loved like this before. Perhaps others have abandoned or hurt you. Remember: "Though my father and mother forsake me, the Lord will receive me" (Psalm 27:10).

Now you know...God loves you! His love is without conditions. It doesn't matter what you've done or if you have made mistakes. His love for you never changes.

"Though my father and mother forsake me, the Lord will receive me."

Psalm 27:10

"After they prayed, the place where they were meeting was shaken. And they were all filled with the Holy Spirit and spoke the word of God boldly."

Acts 4:31

"All of them were filled with the Holy Spirit and began to speak in other tongues…."

Acts 2:4

"But when he, the Spirit of truth, comes, he will guide you into all truth. He will not speak on his own; he will speak only what he hears, and he will tell you what is yet to come."

John 16:13

Filled with the Holy Spirit

"After they prayed, the place where they were meeting was shaken. And they were all filled with the Holy Spirit and spoke the word of God boldly."

Acts 4:31

A. Power to live for Jesus

We need power and courage to talk about Jesus to other people. Therefore, God gave us His Holy Spirit.

"But you will receive power when the Holy Spirit comes on you; and you will be my witnesses…."

Acts 1:8

The Holy Spirit is a gift from God who lives within you. He will give you power to testify about God with boldness. Jesus said:

> "In that day you will no longer ask me anything. Very truly I tell you, my Father will give you whatever you ask in my name."
>
> **John 16:23**

You can be filled with the Holy Spirit…you just have to ask!

B. Pray in a new tongue

> "All of them were filled with the Holy Spirit and began to speak in other tongues…."
>
> **Acts 2:4**

God has a special gift for you—the gift of the baptism of the Holy Spirit. When you are filled with the Holy Spirit, God gives you a language to pray, a language that no man can understand.

Ask Him for this special gift right now!

Begin by praising God for this new gift. You may begin to hear words inside of you that may sound strange to you at first. Just speak them out. The more you say them, the more words He will give you in your new language.

You can pray in the Spirit when you are not sure of how or what to pray.

When praying in the Spirit, we pray God's perfect will, we build our faith, and we make ourselves strong in Jesus.

"But you, dear friends, by building yourselves up in your most holy faith and praying in the Holy Spirit."

Jude 1:20

C. Your guide in life

"But when he, the Spirit of truth, comes, he will guide you into all truth. He will not speak on his own; he will speak only what he hears, and he will tell you what is yet to come."

John 16:13

When you have decisions to make, the Holy Spirit and the Word of God will guide you.

"Your word is a lamp to my feet and a light for my path."

Psalm 119:105

"His divine power has given us everything we need for life and godliness through our knowledge of him…."

2 Peter 1:3

"…by his wounds you have been healed."

1 Peter 2:24

"But seek first his kingdom and his righteousness, and all these things will be given to you as well."

Matthew 6:33

A Life of Blessings

"His divine power has given us everything we need for life and godliness through our knowledge of him…."

2 Peter 1:3

A. God's will is for you to be blessed

God wants us to live abundantly, having more than enough. When God gave His only Son for us, He showed us how He wants us to have everything. "He who did not spare his own Son, but gave him up for us all—how will he not also, along with him, graciously give us all things?" (Romans 8:32).

He wants us to walk in health, provision, joy, peace, and much more. God has already given us all the things we need in life. Now you need to have faith and believe that His promises are true. Walk every day receiving the blessings God wants you to have. The Bible teaches us that He will give us all the things we may need. "And my God will meet all your needs according to the riches of his glory in Christ" (Philippians 4:19).

It doesn't matter what your family's past or current situation may be, God has a life full of blessings if you take His hand and believe by faith that He will give you everything.

B. You can be healed

When Jesus died on the cross, He erased our sins to save our spirit from an eternal death. He also takes good care of our physical body: "I pray that you may enjoy good health..." (3 John 2). God wants you to live a healthy life. Jesus not only died on the cross for our sins, but He also healed us through His wounds. Jesus paid the price so that you can live free of any pain and sickness.

Sometimes you may feel sick. Perhaps people called you "sick," but you must take in faith all God's promises for your life. There is healing power in the Word of God: "He sent out his word and healed them; he rescued them from the grave" (Psalm 107:20).

Speak the Word of God over your life and walk in health. Whenever sickness comes to you, cast it away in the name of Jesus. Use the Bible, read it and confess it. Start receiving God's healing by confessing His Word.

"…by his wounds you have been healed."

1 Peter 2:24

"But seek first his kingdom and his righteousness, and all these things will be given to you as well."

Matthew 6:33

C. Put God 1st

God wants to be first in your life. He wants to have the first place in your heart. Sometimes other people or things have the most important place in your heart, but you must see that only God has the first place.

So when you live to know Him and please Him, all His blessings will be added to your life.

"Take delight in the Lord and he will give you the desires of your heart."

Psalm 37:4

Put God first and you will see your biggest dreams…come true!

"…because the one who is in you is greater than the one who is in the world."

1 John 4:4

"I can do all this through him who gives me strength."

Philippians 4:13

"For the Spirit God gave us does not make us timid, but gives us power, love and self-discipline."

2 Timothy 1:7

"…never will I leave you; never will I forsake you."

Hebrews 13:5

A Life of Victory

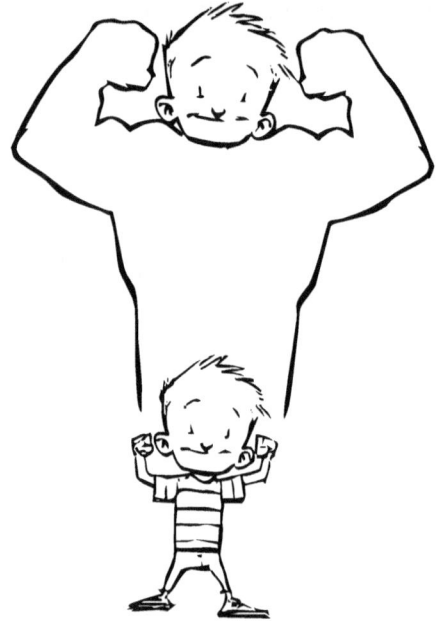

"I can do all this through him who gives me strength."

Philippians 4:13

A. Jesus lives inside of you!

You are a winner because Jesus lives in you! He is more powerful than anything or anyone that may come against you.

> "…because the one who is in you is grater than the one who is in the world."
>
> **1 John 4:4**

It may seem impossible to solve your problems, but the Word of God says:

> "I can do all this through him who gives me strength."
>
> **Philippians 4:13**

B. Do not fear

God doesn't want us to be afraid since He is always with us. "Even though I walk through the darkest valley, I will fear no evil, for you are with me..." (Psalm 23:4).

You don't have to live in fear! God said that He would never leave us. The Lord is your helper; nobody can hurt you. Don't be afraid! You are not alone...God is always with you to protect you!

Whenever you feel scared or feel like you are not able to do certain things, remember...God is by your side and you are not alone.

So, the next time you feel fear in your heart, just say, "Fear, go away in the name of Jesus."

> "For the Spirit God gave us does not make us timid, but gives us power, love and self-discipline."
>
> **2 Timothy 1:7**

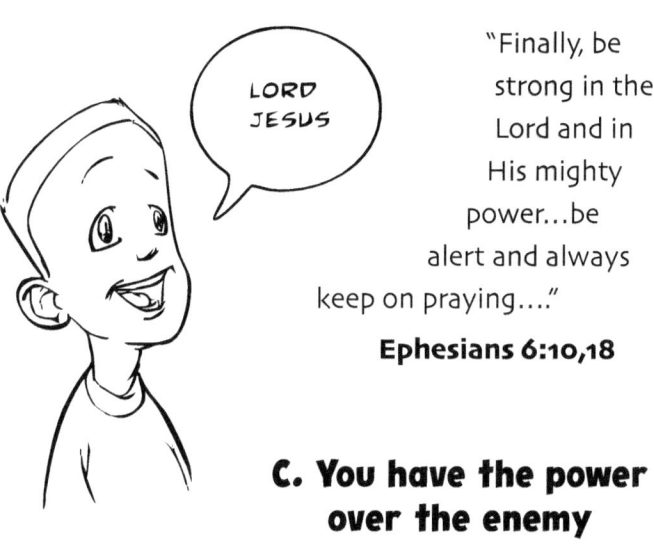

"Finally, be strong in the Lord and in His mighty power…be alert and always keep on praying…."

Ephesians 6:10,18

C. You have the power over the enemy

Don't worry…be happy with all you have because God says in the Bible, "…never will I leave you; never will I forsake you" (Hebrews 13:5).

Jesus has all authority in heaven and earth (Matthew 28:18). Jesus defeated the enemy when He rose from the dead. Jesus said that we have that same power in our life and we could do bigger things than He did. In the name of Jesus you have power over the enemy.

God has given you His armor to fight against the devil's trap.

Use the weapons God has given you!

(Jesus said) "…but whoever loses his life for me and for the gospel will save it."

Mark 8:35

"The Spirit of the Lord is on me, because he has anointed me to preach good news to the poor. He has sent me to proclaim freedom for the prisoners and recovery of sight for the blind, to set the oppressed free, to proclaim the year of the Lord's favor."

Luke 4:18-19

(Jesus said) "…Love one another. As I have loved you…."

John 13:34

You Have a Purpose

A. Give your life

Jesus said: "...but whoever loses his life for me and for the gospel will save it" (Mark 8:35).

When you give your life for Jesus, you find a purpose for it. To give your life means to be willing to do anything because of Jesus. He gave His life because He loves us.

Many people just live to their own pleasures; they just think about themselves until they realize their life has no purpose. There is no better, more wonderful life than serving the living God.

"...if anyone wants to be first, he must be the very last, and the servant of all."

Mark 9:35

B. Tell the good news

"…go into all the world and preach the good news to all creation."

Mark 16:15

There is good news. The good news is that Jesus came to earth, died, rose and now is in heaven helping us to be better…to be GIANTS!

We have been called to share this good news with others. The Holy Spirit is in you! He has already given you the power to preach the good news to heal the hurting, the blind, and to set the captives free.

To preach means to tell others the Word of God and about what Jesus has done in your life. Be brave! Go and tell others about the hope and life in Jesus!

"The Spirit of the Lord is on me, because he has anointed me to preach good news to the poor. He has sent me to proclaim freedom for the prisoners and recovery of sight for the blind, to set the oppressed free, to proclaim the year of the Lord's favor."

Luke 4:18-19

Jesus said: "…Love one another. As I have loved you…."

John 13:34

C. Love and serve

Your purpose in life is to love God and to serve others—to love God with all your heart, soul, mind, and strength.

"Love the Lord your God with all your heart and with all your soul and with all your mind and with all your strength."

Mark 12:30

We are part of God's family, and He wants us to love and serve others just like He has done for us. Jesus also said, "...Love your neighbor as yourself" (Mark 12:31).

Because of love, Jesus came to earth to serve and to give His life for us. We know about His love because He gave His life for us (1 John 3:16). You have been called to give your life so you can "show God's love to others."

We are to love and serve God and others.

You Have a Purpose

The 5 Most Important Things...in All the World!

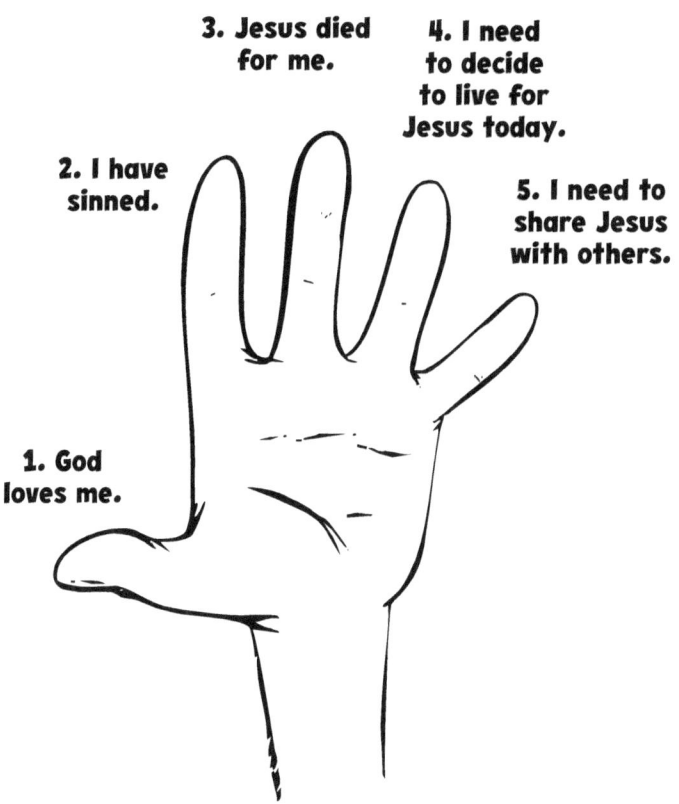

3. Jesus died for me.

4. I need to decide to live for Jesus today.

2. I have sinned.

5. I need to share Jesus with others.

1. God loves me.

Repeat this prayer:

Heavenly Father, I believer You sent Your Son, Jesus, to die on the cross for my sins and that He was raised from the dead.

This day I open my heart to receive You as my Lord, Savior, and Powerful GIANT.

Please forgive my sins and come to live inside me. Thanks for a new life and help me to tell others about You. In Jesus' name. Amen.

How We Grow in Christ

4 steps for you to grow in your walk with Jesus Christ…

1. Pray

Talk to God every day.

2. Read the Bible

There you will find God's promises for you.

3. Go to Church

Praise God along with other believers.

4. Share with Others

Tell others about Jesus.

Today I received Jesus as my Lord and Savior:

Name: _____

Day: _____

Month: _____

Year: _____

About the Author

Rod Baker has served in children's ministry around the world for over 30 years. He is currently the founder and CEO of Bridging Hunger, a food organization dedicated to feeding children while empowering communities to evangelize and disciple them. Rod has previously served as a children's pastor, trained children's ministry leaders, and ministered both to and on behalf of children internationally. He and his wife, Gloria, reside in Jenks, Oklahoma.

To learn more about Bridging Hunger, visit http://www.bridginghunger.com.

To contact Rod Baker or the organization directly, email info@bridginghunger.com.

Equipping Believers to Walk in the Abundant Life
John 10:10b

Connect with us for fresh content and news about forthcoming books from your favorite authors...

www.ingramcontent.com/pod-product-compliance
Lightning Source LLC
LaVergne TN
LVHW021352080426
835508LV00020B/2253